W9-CFV-318

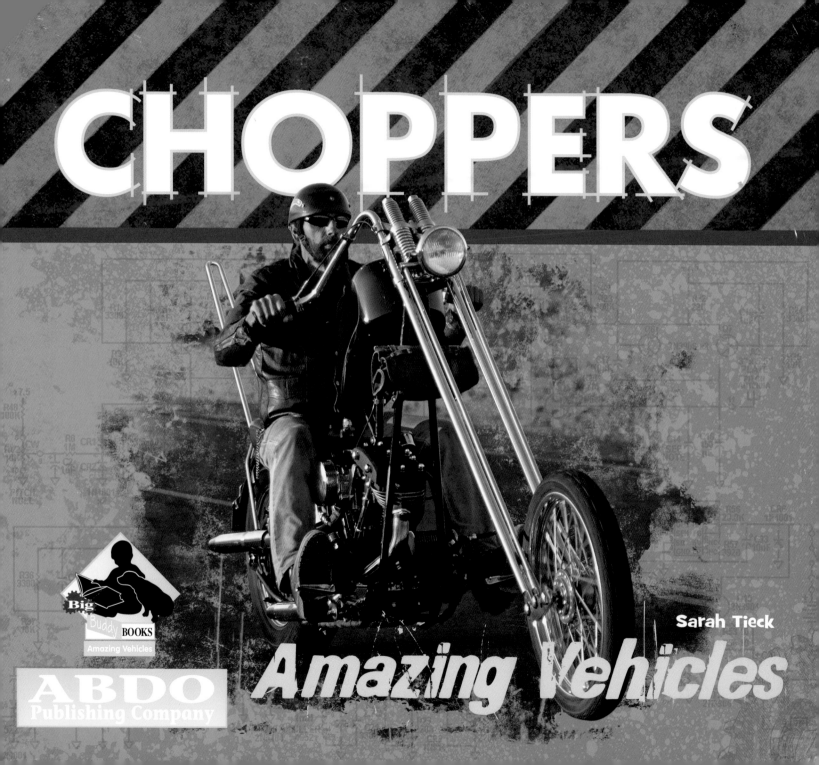

CHOPPERS

Sarah Tieck

Amazing Vehicles

Big Buddy BOOKS
Amazing Vehicles

ABDO
Publishing Company

VISIT US AT
www.abdopublishing.com

Published by ABDO Publishing Company, 8000 West 78th Street, Edina, Minnesota 55439.

Printed in the United States of America, North Mankato, Minnesota.
102010
012011

♻ PRINTED ON RECYCLED PAPER

Coordinating Series Editor: Rochelle Baltzer
Contributing Editors: Megan M. Gunderson, BreAnn Rumsch, Marcia Zappa
Graphic Design: Deb Coldiron, Maria Hosley, Marcia Zappa
Cover Photograph: *iStockphoto*: ©iStockphoto.com/skodonnell.
Interior Photographs/Illustrations: *AP Photo*: Jason Easterly/The Argus-Press (p. 21), Imre Foeldi/MTI/AP (p. 7),
    Morry Gash (p. 23), Tony Gutierrez (p. 25), Osamu Honda (p. 30), Robert E. Klein (pp. 21, 27); *iStockphoto*:
    ©iStockphoto.com/skodonnell (pp. 6, 15, 20, 24, 28); *Getty Images*: Dorling Kindersley (p. 15), Scott Pommier
    (p. 29), Kevin Wintery (p. 5); *Shutterstock*: Steve Adamson (p. 17), David Arts (p. 11), Paul Brennan (p. 7),
    Nikolay Misharev (p. 13), Andrei Oriov (p. 27), REDAV (p. 27), Brad Remy (p. 7), Ljupeo Smokovski (p. 19),
    James Steidl (p. 29), pasphotography (p. 8).

Library of Congress Cataloging-in-Publication Data

Tieck, Sarah, 1976-
 Choppers / Sarah Tieck.
    p. cm. -- (Amazing vehicles)
  ISBN 978-1-61714-695-4
  1. Choppers (Motorcycles)--Juvenile literature. I. Title.
  TL442.7.T54 2011
  629.227'5--dc22
                            2010028576

CONTENTS

GET MOVING

Imagine riding on a chopper. Warm air blows past as you take to the open road. The wheels turn faster and faster over the ground. People are checking out your ride!

Have you ever looked closely at a chopper? Many parts work together to make it move. A chopper is an amazing vehicle!

4

Many choppers are
made to be one of a kind.

WHAT IS A CHOPPER?

A chopper is a motorcycle that has a long frame. Often, choppers are more powerful than standard motorcycles. Choppers may also be **customized** to have a special look. Some people consider building them to be an art form.

There are many types of choppers. They are specially made to help riders show off their style.

A CLOSER LOOK

A chopper has many of the same parts as a standard motorcycle. But, some parts look different. Most choppers have a long fork, a low seat, and wide handlebars.

Some people **customize** choppers from their own ideas. These choppers have special looks. When a chopper is custom-built, it is unlike any other chopper.

 The **fuel tank** is small and often has a special pattern.

 The **handlebars** are called drag bars or ape-hangers.

 Riders rest their feet on small **foot pegs**.

 A chopper's **fork** is long. The front wheel is far from the frame compared to a standard motorcycle.

 A **fender** surrounds the top of one or both wheels. It keeps water and mud from spraying the rider.

HOW DOES IT MOVE?

Like other motorcycles, a chopper moves when its two wheels turn. But, the wheels need power to move!

The chopper's engine supplies that power. It provides enough force to turn an **axle**. This axle is connected to the bike's back wheel. When it turns, the wheels turn.

BITTE NICHT BERÜHREN

THUNDERBIKE

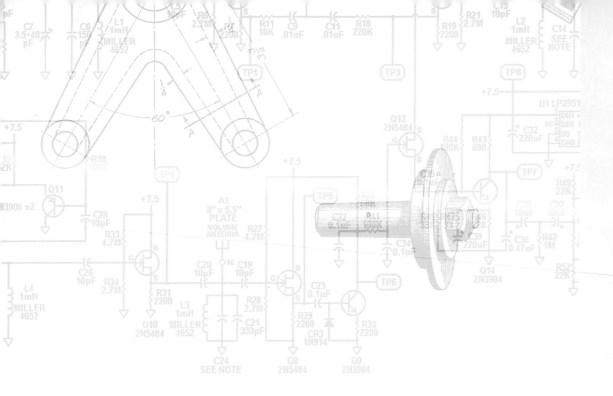

Mirror

A rider uses the handlebars to control the chopper's direction. To turn, the rider leans right or left with the handlebars.

Movable parts, such as front brakes, are on the handlebars. These let the rider change speed. The foot pedal controls the rear brake.

The handlebars have a mirror to help a rider see other vehicles. Just below the handlebars, the speedometer shows how fast the chopper is going.

Speedometer

POWERFUL ENGINES

Most choppers have internal combustion engines. These engines have three main parts. They are the piston, the **cylinder**, and the spark plug.

The piston slides up and down inside the cylinder. It presses a mixture of **fuel** and air together. Then, the spark plug sets the mixture on fire. The burning mixture powers the engine.

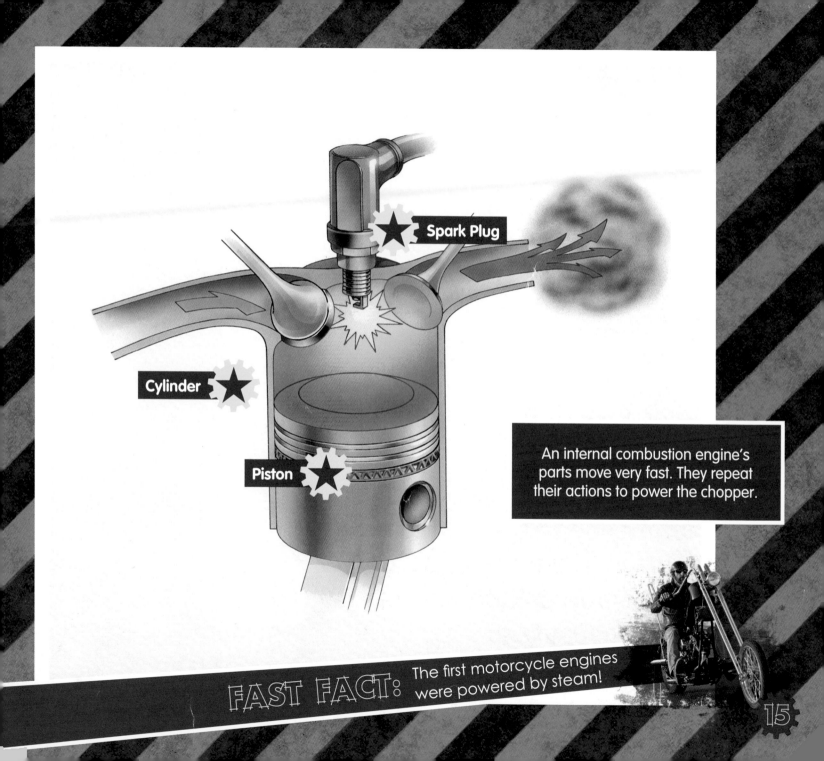

Spark Plug

Cylinder

Piston

An internal combustion engine's parts move very fast. They repeat their actions to power the chopper.

FAST FACT: The first motorcycle engines were powered by steam!

Choppers are made to move fast! For many choppers, powerful V-twin engines make this possible. This type of engine has two **cylinders** placed in a V shape. A chopper's engine is built into its frame.

Harley-Davidson was the first company to use a V-twin engine. Now other motorcycle brands feature this, too. Can you see the V-shaped engine?

THE DRIVER'S SEAT

Choppers are fun and exciting to drive. But, they can also be unsafe. It takes practice and skill to drive them safely. So, every driver must earn a motorcycle **license**.

Most chopper drivers wear special gear to keep safe. They put on helmets and clothes that cover their bodies.

EASY RIDER

It is fun to plan and build a chopper. Many people build their own. Others hire someone to build one for them. They find ideas in books, in magazines, and online.

When a chopper is finished, it's time for the open road! People may ride alone or in groups. Some say they feel free when they are riding choppers.

It may take a team of people to build a chopper. Some people do this work as their job. Others do it as a hobby.

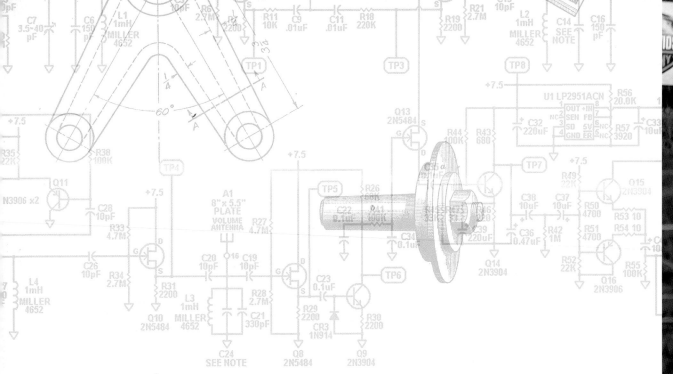

Chopper owners get together and show off their bikes. Sometimes they have shows or events.

One of the most famous motorcycle events happens in Sturgis, South Dakota. Every summer, motorcycle owners from all over the world travel to Sturgis. There, they ride together and check out each other's bikes.

ELCOME RIDERS!

Sturgis is a small city in the Black Hills of South Dakota. Thousands of people fill its streets during the Sturgis Motorcycle Rally!

23

FAST FACT: Motorcycle Mania and Monster Garage are popular television shows about choppers.

CHOPPER MADNESS

Customized motorcycles have been around since **World War II**. At first, people who rode them were considered **rebels**.

Over the years, more and more people learned about choppers. Around 2000, television shows about choppers started. Many people watched these shows and decided they wanted choppers of their own.

The television show *American Chopper* started in 2003. It is about a family business called Orange County Choppers. In it, people build choppers.

ONE OF A KIND

Choppers may have many unusual parts and wild paint jobs. These bikes are more for looks and are not ridden very often.

There are many kinds of choppers. Some choppers are mostly built for looks and style. Almost any part can be **customized**. Drivers may change fenders, seats, **fuel** tanks, or even screws and bolts!

Other choppers are made to be powerful on the road. Lowering the seat gives the driver better control. And a longer front end makes a smoother, faster ride.

Harley-Davidson motorcycles are often made into choppers.

Some choppers have very wide rear wheels. These wheels help the bike ride smoothly.

PAST TO PRESENT

During **World War II**, American soldiers used small, fast bikes in Europe. After the war, they wanted similar bikes at home. So, they began to remove, or "bob," parts from their bikes. These bikes became known as bobbers.

Over time, people chopped and changed the frames of their motorcycles. These bikes became known as choppers. Today, you can see choppers on the open road or on television shows. Choppers are amazing vehicles!

Bobbers are motorcycles that have had parts removed to increase speed. They have an old-fashioned look.

Choppers are motorcycles that have had the frame cut and made longer. They have a modern look.

BLAST FROM THE PAST

One of the most famous choppers is called Captain America. It appeared in a movie in 1969. Captain America got people excited about choppers.

Captain America stood for **rebellion** and freedom. Its **fuel** tank is painted like an American flag. Today, the popular chopper is displayed at the National Motorcycle Museum in Anamosa, Iowa.

IMPORTANT WORDS

axle (AK-suhl) a bar on which a wheel or a pair of wheels turns.

customized (KUHS-tuh-mized) made to be one of a kind.

cylinder (SIH-luhn-duhr) an object that is shaped like a can. The flat ends of a cylinder are circles.

fuel (FYOOL) something burned to give heat or power.

license (LEYE-suhnts) a paper or a card showing that someone is allowed to do something by law.

rebel a person who resists authority. Rebellion is open resistance to authority.

World War II a war fought in Europe, Asia, and Africa from 1939 to 1945.

WEB SITES

To learn more about choppers, visit ABDO Publishing Company online. Web sites about choppers are featured on our Book Links page. These links are routinely monitored and updated to provide the most current information available.

www.abdopublishing.com

INDEX

CLOVER HILL